NIST Technical Note

Using the BACnet Communications DLL v1.0

Michael A. Galler

U.S. DEPARTMENT OF COMMERCE
National Institute of Standards and Technology
Building Environment Division
Building and Fire Research Laboratory
Gaithersburg, Maryland 20899-8631, USA

September 2008

U.S. Department of Commerce
Carlos M. Gutierrez, Secretary

National Institute of Standards and Technology
Patrick D. Gallagher, Deputy Director

ABSTRACT

Using the BACnet Communications DLL v1.0

The BACnet standard defines a communication protocol for information exchange between components of a distributed building automation and control system. The BACnet communications dynamically linked library enables researchers to implement selected BACnet communications, creating an interface for data collection that is easy to use. Researchers can integrate the BACnet communications DLL (Dynamically Linked Library) into existing tools, create a new tool with the BACnet communications DLL (BCD), or use the BCD with common data acquisition and analysis tools. The BCD has already been used to collect data in a variety of locations.

Table of Contents

1. Introduction 1

2. Usage 2

    2.1 Use of the readPVProperty subroutine 3

    2.2 Use of the readObjProperty subroutine...6

    2.3 Use of the writePVProperty subroutine 9

    2.4 Use of the writeObjProperty subroutine 12

    2.5 Use of the BACnetObjectInfo subroutine 15

    2.6 Use of the sendWhoIs subroutine 17

    2.7 Use of the WPCInit and WPCClose subroutines.....................................19

    2.8 Use of the getDefaultAdapter subroutine 20

    2.9 Use of the setDefaultAdapter subroutine...21

    2.10 Use of the getAdapterMAC subroutine 22

3. Extensibility 23

4. Summary...24

5. Future Work 24

6. References...24

1. Introduction

The BACnet standard [1] defines a communication protocol for information exchange between components of a distributed building automation and control system. As BACnet enabled HVAC (Heating, Ventilating, and Air Conditioning) systems have proliferated, so have the possibilities to perform research enabled by access to them from a personal computer or workstation. By accessing HVAC controllers from a computer, the researcher can retrieve data from the BACnet objects on the controllers. This data could include information on the conditions in the building space served by the equipment, the conditions in the equipment itself, the conditions and status of the equipment, the actions the controller is currently taking, and values which may be set by internal program logic. This data can then be used for a variety of research purposes, including real-time monitoring of the HVAC system, fault detection and diagnostics (FDD), data logging, or the application of other types of research tools.

The BACnet communications dynamically linked library (DLL) is designed to simplify communications with BACnet enabled controllers. It allows programs to read and write a variety of values on the controllers, and to implement a range of BACnet commands. The BACnet Communications DLL (BCD) is designed to support data collection from BACnet devices, primarily for use by FDD, data logging, or other similar types of tools, and thus only supports a subset of the capabilities offered by BACnet. The BCD allows communications to any controller accessible from a computer by a local Ethernet (IEEE 802.3) connection. Since it is provided as a DLL, this capability can be integrated into research applications with minimal effort. The BCD can also be accessed by applications commonly used for data acquisition, which are also capable of communicating with a DLL. This allows the same communications code to be used by several applications, each with a different purpose. The BCD was compiled using Microsoft Visual C++ 8.0, and uses the WinPcap 3.1 library [4] for Ethernet communications. The BCD was designed to offer a high degree of functionality and stability, while being flexible and easy to use.

In addition to enabling data acquisition and monitoring, the BCD is intended to be part of a testbed for developing new BACnet objects, properties, and services. It supports communications which allow a program to emulate a BACnet Application Specific Controller (B-ASC), with a goal of allowing emulation of more sophisticated BACnet devices in subsequent versions. The BCD has already been used to collect data in a variety of locations [2,3].

2. Usage

Communications with the BCD is achieved by calling one of a number of subroutines. Each subroutine is designed to perform a specific task with a simple, easy to use interface. The subroutines are divided into three categories: retrieval of data, writing of data, and information retrieval. The available subroutines are listed in Table 2.1.

Table 2.1- Subroutines in the BCD by category

Category	Available Subroutines
Data Retrieval	readPVProperty readObjProperty
Data Writing	writePVProperty writeObjProperty
Network Information	sendWhoIs
Adapter Information	WPCInit/WPCClose getDefaultAdapter setDefaultAdapter getAdapterMAC
BACnet Information	BACnetObjectInfo

The subroutines readPVProperty and readObjProperty are used to retrieve the value of a BACnet property. The value must be represented by a number or a text string. Compound types are not supported, but Boolean and enumerated types are supported. The subroutine readPVProperty could be viewed as a limited case of the readObjProperty subroutine, as it only allows retrieval of the Present_Value BACnet property. It is included to simplify implementation of commonly used functionality. The subroutine readObjProperty allows retrieval of any property of a BACnet object. The subroutines writePVProperty and writeObjProperty are used to write a new value to a property, but otherwise have the same restrictions as their corresponding read subroutines.

Before use, each subroutine must be declared in the code of the calling application using an extern statement. The read- and write- subroutines will initiate one or more BACnet ReadProperty, WriteProperty, ReadPropertyMultiple, or WritePropertyMultiple confirmed service messages to be sent to the appropriate controllers. If a read or write request only has one item, or has consecutive items addressed to different controllers, a ReadPropety or WriteProperty message will be sent. If a request has multiple consecutive items addressed to the same controller, a ReadPropertyMultiple or WritePropertyMultiple message will be sent. The sendWhoIs subroutine will initiate a BACnet Who-Is unconfirmed service message.

2

2.1 Use of the readPVProperty subroutine

2.1.1 Description

Requests for retrieval of the Present_Value property of BACnet objects are implemented by calling the subroutine readPVProperty. Multiple values (up to 250) can be queried with one call to the subroutine. Any type of data that may be stored in the Present_Value property of an allowed object type as shown in Table 2.1.2 can be retrieved, as the values are returned as text strings.

2.1.2 Declaration

The subroutine is declared as:
```
__declspec(dllexport) int readPVProperty( int count, char **devAddr, int
*net, char **router, int *obj, int *inst, char **bv, int *fault);
```

The declaration in the calling program should be:
```
extern __declspec(dllexport) int readPVProperty( int count, char
**devAddr, int *net, char **router, int *obj, int *inst, char **bv, int
*fault);
```

2.1.3 Arguments and Return Value

The arguments to readPVProperty are described in Table 2.1.1 and the values for the obj parameter are given in Table 2.1.2.

Table 2.1.1- Explanation of arguments to the readPVProperty subroutine

Argument	Description
count	The number of values being requested. Each of the other variables should be arrays having this many elements. Accepted values are between 1 and 250.
devAddr	An array of media access control (MAC) addresses. Each MAC address entry is for the BACnet device being queried, not for their routers. The MAC address should be in hexadecimal, and should not be preceded by an 'x' or '0x'. Examples: '0A' or '1A2B3C4D5E6F'.
net	The BACnet network number on which the BACnet device being queried is located, or 0 for the local BACnet network.
router	Router MAC address, if necessary. If there is no router for a query, this should be a string of length 0.
obj	An array of integers representing the BACnet object type of a query (see Table 2.1.2).
inst	An array of integers representing the instance of the BACnet object being queried.
bv	An array of strings holding the requested values (or an error message if there was an error for a particular request).
fault	An array of integers representing the fault status of each request, 1 for no fault or 0 for a fault.

Table 2.1.2- Values for obj argument to the readPVProperty subroutine

Object Type	Argument Value
Analog Input (AI)	0
Analog Output (AO)	1
Analog Value (AV)	2
Binary Input (BI)	3
Binary Output (BO)	4
Binary Value (BV)	5

The return values for readPVProperty are described in Table 2.1.3. Note that a return value indicating a fault may still return some of the requested data, but that one or more values could not be retrieved (i.e., there was a problem with one or more of the requests, but not all of them).

Table 2.1.3- Description of return values for the readPVProperty subroutine.

Return Value	Description
1	No faults returned
0	One or more faults returned. Examine the fault array to determine which request returned a fault.

2.1.4 Example Code
Below are samples of code showing how this subroutine might be implemented. This code is provided for demonstration purposes only.

Single request to device on local network

```
char **devAddr;// to be assigned value "A1B2C3D4E5F6"
int net[1] = { 0 };  // local net
// Note- arrays shown as statically allocated could also be dynamically
allocated
char **router; // to be assigned value  ""
int obj[1] = { 1 };  // Analog Output
int inst[1] = { 5 }; // Instance number 5  (AO5)
char **bv;
int fault[1];
// Allocate memory for devAddr, router, and bv for arrays [1][20]  -
code not shown
// Copy values to devAddr and router - code not shown
int i = readPVProperty (1,devAddr,net,router,obj,inst,bv,fault);  //
count=1 for one value requested
if(i == 0){ } // no errors were found
```

Request two values, from different controllers

```
char **devAddr;// to be assigned values "A1B2C3D4E5F6" and "04"
int net[2] = { 0, 42 };  // local net, and BACnet network 42
char **router; // to be assigned values  "" and "ABCDEF123456"
int obj[2] = { 1, 3 };  // Analog Output and Binary Input
int inst[2] = { 5, 1 }; // Instance number 5  (AO5) and number 1 (BI1)
char **bv;
int fault[2];
// Allocate memory for devAddr, router, and bv for arrays [2][20]  -
code not shown
// Copy values to devAddr and router - code not shown
```

4

```
int i = readPVProperty(2,devAddr,net,router,obj,inst,bv,fault);  //
count=2 for two values requested
```

Request a sequence of values from one controller

```
int count = 10;
char **devAddr;// to be assigned value "A1B2C3D4E5F6" for each item
int net[10];  // local net for each item
char **router; // to be assigned value  "" for each item
int obj[10], inst[10], fault[10];
char **bv;
// Allocate memory for devAddr, router, and bv for arrays [10][20]  -
code not shown
for(int i=0;i< count;i++){
     // Copy values to devAddr, router, net, obj - code not shown
     inst[i] = i+1;  // Object instances 1 to 10
}
int i = readPVProperty(count,devAddr,net,router,obj,inst,bv,fault);  //
count=10 for ten values requested
```

2.2 Use of the readObjProperty subroutine

2.2.1 Description

The subroutine readObjProperty is similar to the subroutine readPVProperty, except that it allows the value of any property to be read, not just Present_Value. The only functional difference is the additional parameters allowing the user to specify the property and (optional) array index being read. This subroutine may also request data from any BACnet object type, not just those to which readPVProperty is limited. The only exception to this is that value of the read property must be represented by a number or a text string. Compound types are not supported, but Boolean and enumerated types are supported. If readObjProperty is called with the Present_Value property specified for each requested item, the result is identical to a call to readPVProperty.

2.2.2 Declaration

The subroutine is declared as:
```
__declspec(dllexport) int readObjProperty( int count, char **devAddr,
int *net, char **router, int *obj, int *inst, int *prop, int *index,
char **bv, int *fault);
```

The declaration in the calling program should be:
```
extern __declspec(dllexport) int readObjProperty( int count, char
**devAddr, int *net, char **router, int *obj, int *inst, int *prop, int
*index, char **bv, int *fault);
```

2.2.3 Arguments and Return Value

The arguments to readObjProperty are described in Table 2.2.1. Note that the arguments are identical to those of the function readPVProperty, except for the new arguments prop and index.

Table 2.2.1- Explanation of arguments to the readObjProperty subroutine

Argument	Description
count	The number of values being requested. Each of the other variables should be arrays having this many elements. Accepted values are between 1 and 250.
devAddr	An array of MAC addresses. Each MAC address entry is for the BACnet device being queried, not for routers. The MAC address should be in hexadecimal, and should not be preceded by an 'x' or '0x'. Examples: '0A' or '1A2B3C4D5E6F'.
net	The BACnet network number on which the BACnet device being queried is located, or 0 for the local BACnet network.
router	Router MAC address, if necessary. If there is no router for a query, this should be a string of length 0.
obj	An array of integers representing the BACnet object type of a query.
inst	An array of integers representing the instance of the BACnet object being queried.
prop	An array of integers representing the property number being queried.
index	An array of integers representing the array index of the BACnet object being queried. This should be set to a value of -1 for each object where an array index is not used.
bv	An array of strings holding the requested values (or an error message if there was an error for a particular request)
fault	An array of integers representing the fault status of each request, 1 for no fault or 0 for a fault.

The return values for readObjProperty are described in Table 2.2.2. Note that a return value indicating a fault does not mean that no values were returned, but that one or more values could not be retrieved.

Table 2.2.2- Description of return values for the readObjProperty subroutine.

Return Value	Description
1	No faults returned
0	One or more faults returned. Examine the fault array to determine which request returned a fault.

2.2.4 Example Code

Below are samples of code showing how this subroutine might be implemented. This code is provided for demonstration purposes only.

Single request to device on local network

```
char **devAddr;// to be assigned value "A1B2C3D4E5F6"
int net[1] = { 0 };  // local net
// Note- arrays shown as statically allocated could also be dynamically
allocated
char **router; // to be assigned value  ""
int obj[1] = { 8 };  // Device object
int fault[1], inst[1] = { 20 }; // Instance number 20
int index[1] = { -1 };  // Not using array instance for this request
int prop[1] = { 70 };  // request the model-name property
char **bv;
// Allocate memory for devAddr, router, and bv for arrays [1][20]  -
code not shown
// Copy values to devAddr and router - code not shown
// Note that count=1 for one value requested
int i =
readObjProperty(1,devAddr,net,router,obj,inst,prop,index,bv,fault);
if(i == 0){ } // no errors were found
```

Request two values, from different controllers

```
char **devAddr;// to be assigned values "A1B2C3D4E5F6" and "04"
int net[2] = { 0, 42 };  // local net, and BACnet network 42
char **router; // to be assigned values  "" and "ABCDEF123456"
int obj[2] = { 1, 3 };  // Analog Output and Binary Input
int inst[2] = { 5, 1 }; // Instance number 5  (AO5) and number 1 (BI1)
int prop[2] = { 85, 85 }; // Present_Value property
int index[1] = { -1, -1 };  // Not using array instance for this request
char **bv;
int fault[2];
// Allocate memory for devAddr, router, and bv for arrays [2][20]  -
code not shown
// Copy values to devAddr and router - code not shown
// Note that count=2 for two values requested
int i =
readObjProperty(2,devAddr,net,router,obj,inst,prop,index,bv,fault);
```

Request a sequence of values from one controller

```
int count = 10;
char **devAddr;// to be assigned value "A1B2C3D4E5F6" for each item
int net[10];  // local net for each item
char **router; // to be assigned value  "" for each item
int obj[10], inst[10], fault[10], prop[10], index[10];
char **bv;
// Allocate memory for devAddr, router, and bv for arrays [10][20]  -
code not shown
for(int i=0;i< count;i++){
    // Copy values to devAddr, router, net, obj, index - code not shown
    inst[i] = i+1;  // Object instances 1 to 10
    prop[i] = 77;   // object-name property
}
// Note that count=10 for ten values requested
int i =
readObjProperty(count,devAddr,net,router,obj,inst,prop,index,bv,fault);
```

2.3 Use of the writePVProperty subroutine

2.3.1 Description

Commands to overwrite the Present_Value property of BACnet objects are implemented by calling the subroutine writePVProperty. Multiple values can be sent with one call to the subroutine. Any type of data that may be written in the Present_Value property of an allowed object type as shown in Table 2.3.2 (i.e., float, int, or Boolean) can be set because the values are sent as text strings.

2.3.2 Declaration

The subroutine is declared as:

```
__declspec(dllexport) int writePVProperty( int count, char **devAddr,
int *net, char **router, int *obj, int *inst, int *prty, char **bv, int
*fault);
```

The declaration in the calling program should be:

```
extern __declspec(dllexport) int writePVProperty( int count, char
**devAddr, int *net, char **router, int *obj, int *inst, int *prty, char
**bv, int *fault);
```

2.3.3 Arguments and Return Value

The arguments to writePVProperty are described in Table 2.3.1 and Table 2.3.2.

Table 2.3.1- Explanation of arguments to the writePVProperty subroutine

Argument	Description
count	The number of values being written. Each of the other variables should be arrays having this many elements. Accepted values are between 1 and 250.
devAddr	An array of MAC addresses. Each MAC address entry is for the BACnet device being contacted, not for routers. The MAC address should be in hexadecimal, and should not be preceded by an 'x' or '0x'. Examples: '0A' or '1A2B3C4D5E6F'.
net	The BACnet network number on which the BACnet device being contacted is located, or 0 for the local BACnet network.
router	Router MAC address, if necessary. If there is no router for a request, this should be a string of length 0.
obj	An array of integers representing the BACnet object type of a request (see Table 2.3.2).
inst	An array of integers representing the instance of the BACnet object being written.
prty	An array of integers representing the priority the value should be written with.
bv	An array of strings holding the values being written to the controller.
fault	An array of integers representing the fault status of each request, 1 for no fault or 0 for a fault.

Table 2.3.2- Values for obj argument to the writePVProperty subroutine

Object Type	Argument Value
Analog Input (AI)	0
Analog Output (AO)	1
Analog Value (AV)	2
Binary Input (BI)	3
Binary Output (BO)	4
Binary Value (BV)	5

The return values for writePVProperty are described in Table 2.3.3. Note that when writing multiple values, when the return value indicates a fault the BCD may still have written some of the requested data, but one or more values could not be written (i.e., there was a problem with one or more of the requests, but not all of them).

Table 2.3.3- Description of return values for the writePVProperty subroutine.

Return Value	Description
1	No faults returned
0	One or more faults returned. Examine the fault array to determine which request returned a fault.

2.3.4 Example Code

Below are samples of code showing how this subroutine might be implemented. This code is provided for demonstration purposes only.

<u>Single request to device on local network</u>

```
char **devAddr;// to be assigned value "A1B2C3D4E5F6"
int net[1] = { 0 };  // local net
// Note- arrays shown as statically allocated could also be dynamically
allocated
char **router; // to be assigned value  ""
int obj[1] = { 1 };  // Analog Output
int inst[1] = { 5 }; // Instance number 5  (AO5)
int prty[1] = { 7 };  // Write at priority 7
char **bv;
int fault[1];
// Allocate memory for devAddr, router, and bv for arrays [1][20]  -
code not shown
// Copy values to devAddr and router – code not shown
int i = writePVProperty (1,devAddr,net,router,obj,inst,prty,bv,fault);
// count=1 for one value requested
if(i == 0){ } // no errors were found
```

<u>Request two values, from different controllers</u>

```
char **devAddr;// to be assigned values "A1B2C3D4E5F6" and "04"
int net[2] = { 0, 42 };  // local net, and BACnet network 42
char **router; // to be assigned values  "" and "ABCDEF123456"
int obj[2] = { 1, 3 };  // Analog Output and Binary Input
int inst[2] = { 5, 1 }; // Instance number 5  (AO5) and number 1 (BI1)
int prty[2] = { 7, 7 };  // Priority of 7
char **bv;
int fault[2];
```

```
// Allocate memory for devAddr, router, and bv for arrays [2][20]  -
code not shown
// Copy values to devAddr and router - code not shown
int i = writePVProperty(2,devAddr,net,router,obj,inst,prty,bv,fault);
// count=2 for two values requested
```

Request a sequence of values from one controller

```
int count = 10;
char **devAddr;// to be assigned value "A1B2C3D4E5F6" for each item
int net[10];  // local net for each item
char **router; // to be assigned value  "" for each item
int obj[10], inst[10], fault[10];
char **bv;
// Allocate memory for devAddr, router, and bv for arrays [10][20]  -
code not shown
for(int i=0;i< count;i++){
     // Copy values to devAddr, router, net, obj - code not shown
     inst[i] = i+1;  // Object instances 1 to 10
}
int i =
writePVProperty(count,devAddr,net,router,obj,inst,prty,bv,fault);
// count=10 for ten values requested
```

2.4 Use of the writeObjProperty subroutine

2.4.1 Description

The subroutine writeObjProperty is similar to the subroutine writePVProperty, except that it allows the value of any property to be written, not just Present_Value. The only functional difference is the additional parameters allowing the user to specify the property and (optional) array index being written. This subroutine may also write data to any BACnet object type, not just those to which writePVProperty is limited. The only exception to this is that value of the written property must be represented by a number or a text string. Compound types are not supported, but Boolean and enumerated types are supported. If writeObjProperty is called with the Present_Value property specified for each requested item, the result is identical to a call to writePVProperty.

2.4.2 Declaration

The subroutine is declared as:

```
__declspec(dllexport) int writeObjProperty( int count, char **devAddr,
int *net, char **router, int *obj, int *inst, int *prop, int *index, int
*prty, char **bv, int *fault);
```

The declaration in the calling program should be:

```
extern      __declspec(dllexport) int writeObjProperty( int count, char
**devAddr, int *net, char **router, int *obj, int *inst, int *prop, int
*index, int *prty, char **bv, int *fault);
```

2.4.3 Arguments and Return Value

The arguments to writeObjProperty are described in Table 2.4.1. Note that the arguments are identical to those of the function writePVProperty, except for the new arguments prop and index.

Table 2.4.1- Explanation of arguments to the writeObjProperty subroutine

Argument	Description
count	The number of values being written. Each of the other variables should be arrays having this many elements. Accepted values are between 1 and 250.
devAddr	An array of Media Access Control (MAC) addresses. Each MAC address entry is for the BACnet device being contacted, not for routers. The MAC address should be in hexadecimal, and should not be preceded by an 'x' or '0x'. Examples: '0A' or '1A2B3C4D5E6F'.
net	The BACnet network number on which the BACnet device being contacted is located, or 0 for the local BACnet network.
router	Router MAC address, if necessary. If there is no router for a request, this should be a string of length 0.
obj	An array of integers representing the BACnet object type of a write request (see Table 2.3.2).
inst	An array of integers representing the instance of the BACnet object being written.
prop	An array of integers representing the property number being written.
index	An array of integers representing the array index of the BACnet object being written. This should be set to a value of -1 for each object where an array index is not used.
prty	An array of integers representing the write priority.
bv	An array of strings holding the values being written to the controller.
fault	An array of integers representing the fault status of each request, 1 for no fault or 0 for a fault.

The return values for writeObjProperty are described in Table 2.4.2. Note that a return value indicating a fault does not mean that no values were written, but that one or more values could not be written.

Table 2.4.2- Description of return values for the writeObjProperty subroutine.

Return Value	Description
1	No faults returned
0	One or more faults returned. Examine the fault array to determine which request returned a fault.

2.4.4 Example Code

Below are samples of code showing how this subroutine might be implemented. This code is provided for demonstration purposes only.

Single request to device on local network

```
char **devAddr;// to be assigned value "A1B2C3D4E5F6"
int net[1] = { 0 };  // local net
// Note- arrays shown as statically allocated could also be dynamically
allocated
char **router; // to be assigned value  ""
int obj[1] = { 8 };  // Device Object
int fault[1], inst[1] = { 20 }; // Instance number 20
int prop[1] = { 85 }; // Present Value
int index[1] = { -1 }; // Index not used
int prty[1] = { 7 };  // Priority of 7
char **bv;
// Allocate memory for devAddr, router, and bv for arrays [1][20]  -
code not shown
// Copy values to devAddr and router - code not shown
int i =
writeObjProperty(1,devAddr,net,router,obj,inst,prop,index,prty,bv,fault)
;
// count=1 for one value requested
if(i == 0){ } // no errors were found
```

Request two values from different controllers

```
char **devAddr;// to be assigned values "A1B2C3D4E5F6" and "04"
int net[2] = { 0, 42 };  // local net, and BACnet network 42
char **router; // to be assigned values  "" and "ABCDEF123456"
int obj[2] = { 1, 3 };  // Analog Output and Binary Input
int inst[2] = { 5, 1 }; // Instance number 5  (AO5) and number 1 (BI1)
int prop[2] = { 85, 85 }; // Present_Value property
int index[2] = { -1, -1 }; // Index not used
int prty[2] = { 7, 7 };  // Priority of 7
char **bv;
int fault[2];
// Allocate memory for devAddr, router, and bv for arrays [2][20]  -
code not shown
// Copy values to devAddr and router - code not shown
int i =
writeObjProperty(2,devAddr,net,router,obj,inst,prop,index,bv,fault);
// count=2 for two values requested
```

Request a sequence of values from one controller

```
int count = 10;
char **devAddr;// to be assigned value "A1B2C3D4E5F6" for each item
int net[10];   // local net for each item
char **router; // to be assigned value  "" for each item
int obj[10], inst[10], fault[10], prop[10], index[10], prty[10];
char **bv;
// Allocate memory for devAddr, router, and bv for arrays [10][20]  -
code not shown
for(int i=0;i< count;i++){
        // Copy values to devAddr, router, index, prty, net, obj -
        // code not shown
        inst[i] = i+1;  // Object instances 1 to 10
        prop[i] = 77;  // object-name property
}
int i =
writeObjProperty(count,devAddr,net,router,obj,inst,prop,index,prty,bv,
fault);
// count=10 for ten values requested
```

2.5 Use of the BACnetObjectInfo subroutine

2.5.1 Description

This subroutine is used to obtain information about BACnet object types supported by the BCD and their properties. It returns information on the set of objects and properties supported by the current version of the BCD. This is valuable to have available dynamically as the list of BACnet objects and properties is periodically revised. Note that future versions of the BCD may have support for draft versions of new BACnet objects, to help fulfill its mission as a research tool. The information that is available includes the number of BACnet object types, the names of the BACnet objects, and the count and names of the properties of each object type. Note that this subroutine does not give information or values from any controllers on the network, or from any specific instance of an object or property on a controller. Use of this subroutine does not generate any messages on the network, or rely on information previously gathered from the network. Information about BACnet objects located on a specific controller can instead be obtained using the readObjProperty subroutine.

2.5.2 Declaration

The subroutine is declared as:
```
__declspec(dllexport) int BACnetObjectInfo (int reqObject,int
reqProp,char *propName);
```

The declaration in the calling program should be:
```
extern __declspec(dllexport) int BACnetObjectInfo (int reqObject,int
reqProp,char *propName);
```

2.5.3 Arguments and Return Value

The arguments to BACnetObjectInfo are described in Table 2.5.1.

Table 2.5.1- Explanation of arguments to the BACnetObjectInfo subroutine

Argument name	Value	Description
reqObject	< 0	Returns the number of BACnet objects
	>= 0	If reqProp is < 0, returns the number of properties for the indicated object, and copies the text name of the indicated object to propName If reqProp is > 0, returns the value 1 and copies the text name of the indicated property to propName. Note that the numbering for BACnet objects starts at 0. If there are N objects, the last one is specified by the value N-1. This is also valid for properties. This is standard for C and C++ programming. If reqObject is a number greater than the number of BACnet objects, an error value of -1 will be returned.
reqProp	< 0	Only evaluated if reqObject refers to a valid object. Returns property count for reqObject.
	>= 0	Only evaluated if reqObject is set to a valid object. Returns text label of reqProp in the propName parameter. If reqProp is a number greater than the number of properties for the indicated BACnet object, an error value of -2 will be returned.
propName		This variable is only used to return text labels of objects or properties. It should be initialized as an array of characters at least 40 characters long.

15

The meaning of the return value depends on which arguments are used. If the reqObject parameter is negative, the return value will be the number of BACnet object types supported. If reqObject is larger than the number of BACnet object types supported, an error value of -1 will be returned. If reqObject is valid and reqProp is negative, the return value will be the number of properties supported by the BACnet object indicated by reqObject. If reqProp is a valid property number, the property name requested will be copied to propName and a value of 1 will be returned. If reqProp is larger than the valid range, an error value of -2 will be returned. The return values are described in Table 2.5.2.

Table 2.5.2- Description of return values for the BACnetObjectInfo subroutine.

Return Value	Description
> 0	The request was returned successfully.
-1	There was an error with the reqObject parameter.
-2	There was an error with the reqProp parameter.

2.5.4 Example Code
Below are samples of code showing how this subroutine might be implemented. This code is provided for demonstration purposes only.

Retrieve the number of BACnet object types supported

```
char opname[40];
int i;

i = BACnetObjectInfo(-1,0,opname);
// note that the value of reqProp will not be evaluated
printf("There are %d BACnet object types supported",i);
```

Retrieve the name of, and the number of properties supported by BACnet, object type 0

```
// note: BACnet object type 0 is analog-input
i = BACnetObjectInfo(0,-1,opname);
//NOTE- opname == "analog-input"
printf("BACnet object type 0 is named %s",opname);
printf("BACnet object type 0 has %d properties",i);
```

Retrieve the name of a specific property of BACnet object type 0 (analog-input)

```
i = BACnetObjectInfo(0,5,opname);
// NOTE- opname == "status-flags"
printf("Property 5 ofBACnet object type 0 is labeled '%s'",opname);
```

2.6 Use of the sendWhoIs subroutine

2.6.1 Description

The sendWhoIs subroutine is used to obtain a listing of BACnet devices that are on the BACnet internetwork, and on locally connected networks. It can be used to detect all devices, or it can be used to do a limited search based on Device object instance number ranges. It works by sending a global BACnet WhoIs request.

2.6.2 Declaration

The subroutine is declared as:

```
__declspec(dllexport) int sendWhoIs(char **devAddr, char **router, int
*net, int *devid, int max=100, int low=-1, int high=-1);
```

The subroutine should be declared in the calling program as follows:

```
extern __declspec(dllexport) int sendWhoIs(char **devAddr, char
**router, int *net, int *devid, int max=100, int low=-1, int high=-1);
```

Note the default values provided for the max, low, and high parameters. The variables devAddr, router, net, and devid are arrays which are filled with return values by sendWhoIs. If the value of the max variable is not specified, it is important that the arrays which have return values in them are allocated with a sufficient length (i.e., at least a length of 100).

2.6.3 Arguments and Return Value

The arguments to sendWhoIs are described in Table 2.6.1.

Table 2.6.1- Explanation of arguments to the sendWhoIs subroutine

Argument	Value	Description
devAddr	NA	Returns text labels of MAC addresses of found devices. It should be initialized as an array of characters at least 15 characters long.
router	NA	Returns text labels of MAC addresses of routers to found devices. If a device has no router, this will return a string of length 0. It should be initialized as an array of characters at least 15 characters long.
net	NA	Returns text labels of the BACnet network number of each found device.
devid	NA	Returns text labels of the device object instance number for each found device.
max	> 0	Optional; Mmaximum number of found devices for which information should be returned. This number should be the same as the length of the arrays for devAddr, router, net, and devid. This variable has a default value of 100.
low	>= 0 and <= high	Optional; Specifies the low end when searching for device objects with instance numbers in a specific range. If used, the variables max and high must also be specified. If passed with a value of -1, this parameter and the high parameter will be ignored.
high	>= low and <= 4,194,303	Optional; Specifies the high end when searching for Device object with instance numbers in a specific range. If used, the variables low and high must also be specified.

17

The return value of sendWhoIs will be the number of devices found from the request. This will be zero if no devices responded to the request. If there is an error with one or more of the arguments, the return value will be -1. The return values are described in Table 2.6.2.

Table 2.6.2- Description of return values for the sendWhoIs subroutine.

Return Value	Description
>= 0 and <= max	The number of devices which responded to the request.
-1	There was an error with one or more of the parameters.

2.6.4 Example Code
Below are samples of code showing how this subroutine might be implemented. This code is for demonstration purposes only.

Obtain information about devices on local network

```
char **devAddr, **router;
int *net, *devid ;
int max = 200, low = -1, high = -1;

// Allocate memory for devAddr, router, net and devid arrays to length
max  - code not shown
int devCount = sendWhoIs(devAddr,router,net,devid,max,low,high);  //
request all devices to respond
if(devCount > 0){  // information about devices was returned
    for(i=0;i<devCount;i++)
        printf("Found device with address  %s OBJ ID %d on BACnet network
%d\n", devAddr[i], devid[i], net[i]);
} else {
    printf("There was an error with sendWhoIs( )!\n");
}
```

18

2.7 Use of the WPCInit and WPCClose subroutines

2.7.1 Description

The WPCInit subroutine is used to explicitly initialize the WinPCap connection. If this function is not called explicitly by the calling program, it will be called by the first read or write subroutine called. When called, it will return the number of network adapters present on the computer. If there are multiple adapters present, it will also select the first one with a valid Ethernet address. Note that it will automatically skip modems and some virtual network adapters. A virtual network adapter can be set as the default adapter by calling the setDefaultAdapter subroutine with the appropriate adapter identifier.

The WPCClose subroutine is used to close the WinPCap connections. It will be called automatically by the BCD when it closes, but it may also be called explicitly. This might be useful if a program does not need to send or receive further BACnet packets, but has other processing to finish.

2.7.2 Declaration

The WPCInit subroutine is declared as:
```
__declspec(dllexport) int WPCInit(void);
```

The WPCInit subroutine should be declared in the calling program as follows:
```
extern __declspec(dllexport) int WPCInit(void);
```

The WPCClose subroutine is declared as:
```
__declspec(dllexport) void WPCClose(void);
```

The WPCClose subroutine should be declared in the calling program as follows:
```
extern __declspec(dllexport) void WPCClose(void);
```

2.7.3 Arguments and Return Value

There are no arguments passed to the WPCInit subroutine. The return values are described in Table 2.7.1.

Table 2.7.1- Description of return values for the WPCInit subroutine.

Return Value	Description
< 0	An error occurred with WinPCap.
>= 0	The count of adapters found on the system

There are no arguments to or return values from the WPCClose subroutine.

2.7.4 Example Code

Below are samples of code showing how this subroutine might be implemented. This code is provided for demonstration purposes only.

Initialize WinPCap and get the number of adapters

```
int count;
count = WPCInit();
if(count < 0){      printf("There was an error initializing WinPCap.\n");
} else {            printf("There are %d adapters on this
computer\n",count);}
/* ... */
WPCClose();
```

2.8 Use of the getDefaultAdapter subroutine

2.8.1 Description

The getDefaultAdapter subroutine is used to get the identifier for the current default adapter. Note that numbering starts at 0.

2.8.2 Declaration

The getDefaultAdapter subroutine is declared as:
```
__declspec(dllexport) int getDefaultAdapter(void);
```

The subroutine should be declared in the calling program as follows:
```
extern __declspec(dllexport) int getDefaultAdapter(void);
```

2.8.3 Arguments and Return Value

There are no arguments passed to getDefaultAdapter. The return values are described in Table 2.8.1.

Table 2.8.1- Description of return values for the getDefaultAdapter subroutine.

Return Value	Description
< 0	The default adapter has not been set
>= 0	The identifier of the default adapter

2.8.4 Example Code

Below are samples of code showing how this subroutine might be implemented. This code is provided for demonstration purposes only.

Initialize WinPCap and get default adapter identifier

```
int count, adapter_id;

count = WPCInit();

if(count < 0){
     printf("There was an error initializing WinPCap.\n");
} else {
     printf("There are %d adapters on this computer\n", count);
}

adapter_id = getDefaultAdapter( );
printf("The default adapter ID is %d\n", adapter_id);  // this will be 0
if there is only one adapter
```

2.9 Use of the setDefaultAdapter subroutine

2.9.1 Description

The setDefaultAdapter subroutine is used to select the identifier for the current default adapter. Note that numbering starts at 0.

2.9.2 Declaration

The setDefaultAdapter subroutine is declared as:
```
__declspec(dllexport) int setDefaultAdapter(int i);
```

The subroutine should be declared in the calling program as follows:
```
extern __declspec(dllexport) int setDefaultAdapter(int i);
```

2.9.3 Arguments and Return Value

There is one argument passed to setDefaultAdapter, which is the ID of the new default adapter. This must be a valid adapter ID, which is a nonnegative integer, and less than the adapter count as returned by WPCInit. The return values are described in Table 2.9.1.

Table 2.9.1- Description of return values for the setDefaultAdapter subroutine.

Return Value	Description
0	There was an error setting the default adapter
1	The default adapter was set to the new value

2.9.4 Example Code

Below are samples of code showing how this subroutine might be implemented. This code is provided for demonstration purposes only.

Initialize WinPCap and set default adapter ID

```
int count, adapter_id, status;

count = WPCInit();

if(count < 0){
      printf("There was an error initializing WinPCap.\n");
} else {
      printf("There are %d adapters on this computer\n", count);
}

adapter_id = getDefaultAdapter( );
printf("The default adapter ID is %d\n", adapter_id);  // this will be 0
if there is only one adapter
//For this example, let count=3, and the default adapter is 0
status = setDefaultAdapter(1);
if(status == 1){
      printf("The default adapter was changed successfully\n");
} else {
      printf("There was an error setting the default adapter\n");
}
```

2.10 Use of the getAdapterMAC subroutine
2.10.1 Description
The getAdapterMAC subroutine is used to obtain the MAC address of a network adapter.

2.10.2 Declaration
The getAdapterMAC subroutine is declared as:
```
__declspec(dllexport) int getAdapterMAC(int id, unsigned char *label);
```

The subroutine should be declared in the calling program as follows:
```
extern __declspec(dllexport) int getAdapterMAC(int id, unsigned char
*label);
```

2.10.3 Arguments and Return Value
The getAdapterMAC subroutine requires two parameters. The first parameter specifies which adapter is being queried. If this parameter is passed as -1, then the default adapter is used. The second parameter is an output parameter, and will have the MAC address of the adapter copied to it by the getAdapterMAC subroutine. There must be enough space allocated for a MAC address to be copied to this parameter. Note that the MAC address is in unsigned char, not in a human readable format, and will only require a string length of 6 unsigned chars to be allocated. The return values for the getAdapterMAC subroutine are summarized in Table 2.10.1.

Table 2.10.1- Description of return values for the getAdapterMAC subroutine.

Return Value	Description
0	There was an error with an input parameter: the adapter id was out of range, or the label parameter was not allocated
1	No error- the MAC address was copied to the output parameter.

2.10.4 Example Code
Below are samples of code showing how this subroutine might be implemented. This code is provided for demonstration purposes only.

<u>Initialize WinPCap and get the MAC address for the default adapter</u>

```
int count, adapter_id, status;
unsigned char label[6];

count = WPCInit();
if(count < 0){
      printf("There was an error initializing WinPCap.\n");
} else {
      printf("There are %d adapters on this computer\n", count);
}

adapter_id = getDefaultAdapter( );
printf("The default adapter ID is %d\n", adapter_id);  // this will be 0
if there is only one adapter
status = getAdapterMAC(adapter_id, &label);
if(status == 1){ printf("The adapter MAC address was retrieved\n");
else printf("There was an error retrieving the adapter MAC address.\n");
```

22

3. Extensibility

The BACnet standard periodically undergoes revisions, often resulting in changes to the objects, properties, and other entities described by the standard. The standard also permits proprietary extensions. The BCD can be updated to implement changes in enumerated lists, including the addition of proprietary lists, by editing the file bacdll2.xml, which contains every extensible enumerated list defined by the BACnet standard (2004) and addenda A through O (2004). An example showing a modification to the standard from an addendum, and a proprietary modification, is shown below.

```
<enumList label="BACnetSilencedState" listCount="6" extensible="y"
extMin="64" extMax="65535" >
    <enumItem label="unsilenced" id="0" />
    <enumItem label="audible-silenced" id="1" />
    <enumItem label="visible-silenced" id="2" />
    <enumItem label="all-silenced" id="3" />
    <enumItem label="new-silenced-from-addendum" id="4" />
    <enumItem label="proprietary-silenced" id="64" />
</enumList>
```

Enumerated lists are stored in XML format in an "enumList" tag. If an enumList has the property "extensible" with a value of "y" as in the example above, then it is extensible and may have proprietary items added to it. New items should have an id value in the range given by the values of the "extMin" and "extMax" properties, and should otherwise follow the format given in the example above.

4. Summary

The BACnetCommunications DLL enables programmers of HVAC related computer programs to easily incorporate BACnet communications into their tools. It supports a command set that enables the most common types of communications used in data acquisition, monitoring, FDD, or other activities which require communicating with a BACnet enabled device. Use of the BACnet DLL removes a significant barrier to entry for users who wish to write tools but do not have the programming experience to implement the BACnet protocol.

5. Future Work

While the BCD is already capable of being useful in a wide variety of applications, as BACnet expands there will be more places the BCD can be used. Some planned extensions of the BCD are inclusion of a Web Services interface, addition of new BACnet objects and properties, establishment of BACnet/IP communications through the simplified interface, and extensions of simplified interface to include new functionality.

6. References

[1] ASHRAE, ANSI/ASHRAE 135-2004, *BACnet: A Data Communication Protocol for Building Automation and Control Networks*. American Society of Heating, Refrigerating, and Air-Conditioning Engineers Inc. Atlanta, GA.

[2] Bushby, S.T., Castro, N.S., Galler, M.A., Park, C., House, J.M., 2001, "Using the Virtual Cybernetic Building Testbed and FDD Test Shell for FDD Tool Development", NISTIR 6818.

[3] Castro, N.S., Schein, J., Park, C., Galler, M.A., Bushby, S.T., House, J.M., 2003, "Results from Simulation and Laboratory Testing of Air Handling Unit and Variable Air Volume Box Diagnostic Tools", NISTIR 6964.

[4] http://www.winpcap.org